CONTENTS

THIS

Words and Music by DARIUS RUCKER,
FRANK ROGERS and KARA DioGUARDI

Moderately fast

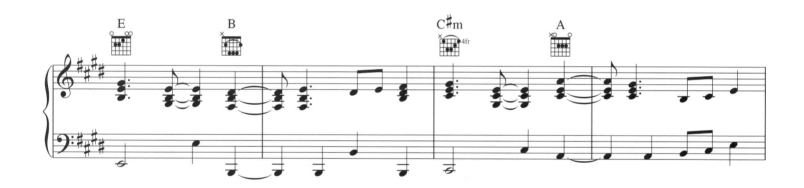

Got a

COME BACK SONG

Words and Music by DARIUS RUCKER,
CASEY BEATHARD and CHRIS STAPLETON

I woke up _____ a-gain _____ this morn-ing
I know I said _____ I would-n't miss _____ you,

and would-n't you know _____ it pour-ing rain. _____
but now _____ I'm say-ing I'm _____ a fool. _____

MIGHT GET LUCKY

Words and Music by DARIUS RUCKER,
RADNEY FOSTER and JAY CLEMENTI

set a - side time __ to get to know each oth - er a - gain. __

And if I play my cards right, __ I know it sounds kind - a

fun - ny, but I might get luck - y.

D.S. al Coda

There's a

CODA

luck - y. __

WHISKEY AND YOU

Words and Music by DARIUS RUCKER
and FRANK ROGERS

SOUTHERN STATE OF MIND

Words and Music by DARIUS RUCKER,
CHRIS DuBOIS and ASHLEY GORLEY

I was up in New York City just the oth-er week.

* Recorded a half step higher.

south - ern   state ___ of   mind. ___

D.S. al Coda

LOVE WILL DO THAT

Words and Music by DARIUS RUCKER,
FRANK ROGERS and DON SAMPSON

THE CRAZIEST THING

Words and Music by DARIUS RUCKER,
MONTY CRISWELL and FRANK ROGERS

Left ____ the bright lights, drove down ____ ____ nine-ty-five ____ to a sleep-y south-ern town. Gave up ____ ____ a sweet gig to have ____ a cou-ple kids, chas-in' her a-round. All ____ her friends ____ roll their eyes and grin ____ when she says ____

THINGS I'D NEVER DO

Words and Music by DARIUS RUCKER,
CLAY MILLS and FRANK ROGERS

that cut ___ just like ___ a blade ___ and leave you dy - in', cry -

D.S. al Coda

- in' all a - lone. _____ But here I

CODA

Oh, ___ I'd nev - er do.

WE ALL FALL DOWN

Words and Music by DARIUS RUCKER
and KIM TRIBBLE

I DON'T CARE

Words and Music by DARIUS RUCKER,
CHRIS DuBOIS and BRAD PAISLEY

Is ten o' clock in the morn - in' too ear - ly to drink beer? ___
(Spoken:) Hey, man, you think those are real or do you think they're fake? You mean those right there? ___

78

SHE'S BEAUTIFUL

Words and Music by DARIUS RUCKER,
FRANK ROGERS and BRETT JONES

She's beau - ti - ful ____ like that. ____

I GOT NOTHIN'

Words and Music by DARIUS RUCKER
and CLAY MILLS

IN A BIG WAY

Words and Music by DARIUS RUCKER
and CASEY BEATHARD

Recorded a half step lower.